CATS

CATS

Joyce Robins

‖ •PARRAGON• ‖

Acknowledgements

Animals Unlimited pages 19, 23, 29, 58, 69; **Bruce Coleman Ltd/Thomas Buchholz** page 56; /**Jane Burton** pages 13, 14–15, 16, 26, 31, 44, 46, 47, 48, 49, 51, 52, 53, 59, 62, 63, 75, 76; /**Erich Crichton** page 17; /**Harald Lange** pages 34, 66; /**Werner Layer** pages 40, 71; /**Andy Price** page 54; /**Hans Reinhard** pages 6, 9, 20, 25, 32, 36, 37, 39, 41, 42, 57, 61, 64, 70, 72–73, 78; /**Kim Taylor** pages 10, 22, 65; **Natural History Photographic Agency/E.A. Janes** jacket; **Sally Anne Thompson/Animal Photography** page 12;

First published in Great Britain in 1994 by
Parragon Book Service Ltd
Units 13-17, Avonbridge Trading Estate
Atlantic Road, Avonmouth
Bristol BS11 9QD

Publishing Manager: Sally Harper
Editor: Anne Crane
Design: Robert Mathias/Helen Mathias

ISBN 1 85813 861 2

Printed in Italy

Contents

CHAPTER ONE

Cat About the House

FACING PAGE: *For all their aloofness, cats can be quite irresistible – as they themselves know so well.*

There are few experiences more pleasurable than nursing a purring cat, as it stretches languidly or curls into an ecstatic ball on your lap. There is no need for tranquillizers or relaxation classes, a quiet cuddle with your cat and the rhythmic stroking of its silky fur is all that is needed to soothe away worries and spread contentment. Books advising on successful home selling often recommend borrowing a cat to sit in front of the fire before prospective buyers arrive, because it will give the house a homely, welcoming feel.

New owners may opt for a cat because it does not demand 'walkies', will not disturb the neighbours or knock over the toddlers but once the cat is ensconced in the household, few people fail to fall under the spell of this graceful, sensuous animal. Though the cat quickly becomes a member of the family, it always retains the slight air of mystery which is part of its fascination.

Cats have a long-standing reputation for being independent and self-seeking which often amuses owners whose pets wind in and out of their legs in a figure of eight the moment they step through the door, determinedly nose aside any obstacles, such as newspapers, books, knitting or even meal trays in the urgent need of a loving lap, or sit on their shoulders drooling with sheer delight. Cats do vary in their need for human contact but, on the whole, you will get from the relationship exactly what you put into it.

Unlike dogs, who have an instinctive devotion to their pack leader, a cat will adapt its expectations and behaviour to correspond with yours. If your cat only shows affection when a meal is in the offing, it may well be that this is the only time it feels the centre of attention. If you are out all day and busy all evening, your cat will make its own amusements and become fairly self-sufficient – though you might well ask yourself why you are keeping a cat at all. If you treat your cat as a companion, it will look to you for love and comfort, fun and games, and will want to poke its whiskers into everything you do. However, you should never take a cat for granted. They are skilled at organizing extra treats and comforts for themselves and, if they have freedom to roam the neighbourhood, they may line up a support system of friendly humans to provide life's little extras – leftover scrambled egg here, a juicy liver morsel there, or perhaps a warm spot in front of an open fire on chilly afternoons, or simply a bit of company while its owner is at work.

A doctor friend, owner of Samantha, made a house call on an elderly patient and was astonished to find her cat looking out of a smart 'igloo' by the radiator, a half-eaten dish of pilchards by her side, and answering to the name of Fred. Samantha was always home for supper with her owner but had found a way of upgrading her lifestyle.

Cat as owner

Some cats are even less subtle about it like Prudence, a 12-year-old tortoiseshell who lived next door to our weekend home several years ago. Her standard of living was not what it had been, as she had been pushed down in the family hierarchy by the arrival of a baby and then a dog. At first, she used to crawl into our house on her tummy, nervous but ingratiating. We were welcoming but firm about putting her out after a short visit, when she would sit crying piteously on the doorstep. Before long she was a regular weekend guest. The moment our car turned into the drive, she was over the fence and was always first into the house, where she took up position in front of an armchair, waiting for someone to provide a lap. She refused to venture out during the weekend, presumably determined to make the most of a good thing, and when we left we had to evict her bodily, hissing and growling in protest.

FACING PAGE: *A cat can become quite self-sufficient, to the extent of having two (or even three) houses to call home.*

LEFT: *Dilated pupils may signal a range of reactions, from fear and wariness to excitement or anticipation.*

Many cat enthusiasts, on the receiving end of imperious feline ways, maintain that 'you can't *own* a cat'. Whatever the truth of this might be, your cat will certainly consider that it owns you. A dog will greet a returning owner with a display of joy, barking and tail wagging, leaping and capering. A cat will rub its head and the side of its face against your leg over and over again, then rub along the whole length of its body until its tail curls around you. If you bend down it will repeat the rubbing against your hand or even your face. This is not just a greeting; the cat is marking you with its own pheromones, from scent glands around its mouth, on its forehead and at the base of its tail, so every movement says 'Mine, mine, mine'.

When you have been out of the house for a while, the scent fades, so the cat needs to 'mark' you all over again, reinforcing its ownership and its sense of security. The frequent marking rituals probably hold the explanation for the frosty reception given to owners returning from holiday. Many people think that the cat is punishing them for their desertion when it stares coolly from its basket or draws back from an outstretched hand but it is more likely that, though your appearance and voice are familiar, you don't smell quite right and the cat needs a short time to adjust.

Body signals

A cat gives off clear signals about its moods and wants with its eyes, ears and tail. When it is frightened, excited or wary, its pupils dilate until its eyes look almost entirely black. This is also a sign of anticipation; a hungry cat will sit beside your armchair fixing you with a black-eyed gaze, as if trying to mesmerize you into going into the kitchen. When strangers are present, the cat's eyes will be wide open, the degree of wariness it is feeling showing in the size of the pupil. Once it feels relaxed and reassured, the eyes will be half closed, the pupils shrinking to small slits. A long slow blink is a sign of recognition given to a trusted friend, and if you want to join in cat talk, try using a slow blink yourself, instead of words.

A peaceful cat holds its ears upwards and slightly sideways but the moment something catches its attention, the ears are pricked and point forwards, ready to

take in the slightest sound. Anxiety or frustration may cause the ears to twitch or the tip of the tail to flick up and down. Tail twitching is usually thought to be a sign of annoyance but it can also be a sign of indecision. When a cat that has been dozing happily on your lap starts to flick the tip of its tail, it is trying to make up its mind about leaving.

There is no mistaking the signals given by the violently swirling or thumping tail of an angry cat, or by an anxious submissive cat when it tucks its tail down between its legs. If a cat comes towards you with a tail held straight up and the tip crooked over it is friendly and curious, and if the tip points straight up in the air, the cat is greeting you with open delight.

When a cat confronts an unwelcome intruder, it uses a whole range of threatening signals. First, it will freeze and stare menacingly, then, if the stranger moves close, the cat will turn sideways to present the largest possible obstacle, arching its

LEFT: *This cat's tail is curled at the tip, signalling a friendly curiosity.*

body and fluffing up the hair along the spine and tail, so that it looks large and fierce. Its legs become stiff and tense, partly to make the cat appear taller and partly so it is ready to leap backwards or forwards, as the situation demands. All the while its teeth are bared and it is giving out a fearsome yowl.

Understanding every word

Cats have a remarkable range of sounds to make their meaning clear, from the gentle trilling noise used by a mother with her kittens, to the bloodcurdling yowls of two cats fighting for supremacy. Some cats are more chatty than others but most develop their own set of distinctive sounds: the plaintive plea for food, the hopeful invitation to play, the anxious bid for reassurance. In oriental cats, particularly, individual voice patterns are so distinctive that owners can pick out their cat's call from among any number of others.

Experts are still arguing over the mechanism of the purring sound, but to cat lovers the scientific explanation is less important than the sheer joy that the sound brings. There is nothing more

ABOVE: *It seems that this apricot tabby kitten is using its voice to send out a distress signal.*

13

comforting, more likely to reassure us that all is right with the world, than a full-throated feline purr. It may come as a surprise to realize that purring is not restricted to happy animals. Cats also purr when they are ill or in pain and even when they confront a more powerful enemy. In these situations, it seems that the purr is used as a signal that all the cat requires is to be left alone, that it wants no trouble and is no threat to anyone.

Close companions

As a cat lies purring on your lap, it will probably knead you in a steady rhythm with its front paws. Unfortunately, sharp claws can make this quite a painful experience but if you push the cat hastily away, it will be bewildered and hurt. As a kitten, it used this trampling motion on its mother's body at feeding time to stimulate the milk supply, and the warmth and security of a cuddle on a comfortable lap has brought back all the pleasure and intimacy of that early time, so it is treating you as a surrogate mother, which most loving owners regard as a great compliment.

One aspect of body language that is frequently misunderstood is the message given by a pet cat as it rolls on its back with its feet in the air and its tummy exposed. This is the cat it its most vulnerable, with its underside unprotected, so it is a gesture showing great trust in its human family. A cat with a nervous temperament will probably never put itself in this position. The obvious temptation is to bend down and stroke the displayed tummy but this will often trigger an automatic defensive reaction in the cat, which may quickly roll over so that its back is uppermost, or close its paws, and even its claws, on your hand to prevent the contact. A cat in real harmony with its owner will allow such a caress, but even then it will probably tolerate, rather than enjoy, the touch.

When you have a close understanding with your cat, it goes both ways and your cat will probably know just how to manipulate you. It will know exactly what form of behaviour will grab your attention,

RIGHT: *With its stomach exposed, the cat is at its most vulnerable.*

however busy you are. Whenever a friend's cat, Lobo, felt neglected, he would jump onto the mantelpiece, wait until he caught his owner's eye, then begin to squeeze his body behind a favourite ornament until it teetered on the edge of the shelf. At all other times, he was perfectly capable of picking his way round ornaments on sure and delicate feet but he knew just what he needed to do to attract her attention and, like a naughty child, he preferred angry attention to no attention at all.

Food is the area where most cats manage to fool their owners. We all know that wide-eyed, affronted 'You don't expect me to eat *that*, do you?' look, followed by a disdainfully shaken back leg and a dignified exit. Pretence of a delicate stomach and exclusive tastebuds has earned many a cat a gourmet menu. When Montmorency went missing for three weeks after moving to a new area, his owner was distraught: he was so fussy he would *never* touch *anything* but freshly cooked chicken or fish, so he was bound to starve to death. When he was brought home in response to newspaper advertisements, he was sleek and healthy, though the family who found him wan-

LEFT: *If it is brought up with dogs, a cat may lose its natural fear of its traditional enemy.*

dering fed him nothing but the cheapest brand of tinned food, along with their three cats. They were astonished to hear that he was a finicky cat; he had always cleaned his bowl before the other cats had a chance to help themselves. On his first night home, Montmorency gazed appalled at a plate of cat food, then walked away with the air of one who would rather starve. Within half an hour, a cod fillet poached in milk was put before him – and if a cat ever smirked, it must have been Montmorency at that moment.

Mixing in

Cats are considered solitary creatures but, given the chance, they often settle very happily into a family of assorted animals. Though dogs are their natural enemies, the cat's speed and agility give it a natural advantage. A cat on its home territory usually puts a pushy dog in its place very quickly, and few dogs take a predatory interest in a cat that does not run away. Some dogs snuggle down to sleep with a feline friend and become very protective. A cat will be able to tell the bark of its family dog from all others but there is a

danger that a cat brought up with dogs will lose some of its natural fear and become complacent. Two of our neighbourhood cats were playing on the lawn when a fierce terrier came bounding towards them. One cat, viewing all dogs as a mortal threat, was off like a rocket, but the other, well used to a houseful of playful dogs, stopped to wonder what the new visitor wanted and was badly injured by snapping jaws.

Two cats in the same household may be

ABOVE: *Cats are just as selective in choosing their friends as humans are.*

lifelong friends but there are no guarantees. I know a family where six pedigree cats – Siamese, Abyssinians and a Rex – sleep in a heap, paws intertwined and faces resting against one another, and another where two Siamese refuse to stay in the same room with one another. Cats are just as picky about their friends as humans; not many of us would set up house for life with a complete stranger and expect to become soul mates. Even if you have brought in a second cat because the first is bored and lonely, it will see the newcomer not as a potential playmate but as a threat to its home comforts, and there will be plenty of hissing, growling and ear-boxing before they sort out their positions in the household. After that, they may become inseparable companions or they may simply learn to tolerate one another.

Trainable cats

There are those who maintain that it is impossible to train cats – and those who have proved them wrong. In fact, cats take very easily to some forms of training. It usually takes very little effort to educate them in the use of the litter tray, but then we are exploiting a cat's natural liking for cleanliness and neat routine. Most cats will become accustomed to a harness, so that they can take their owners for a walk – but woe betide the owners who try to take the cat where it does not want to go. In Britain during the decade from 1966 to 1975, a cat called Arthur made himself and a certain brand of cat food famous by eating daintily from the tin with his paw, a trick which is part of the standard repertoire of trainers.

Experienced trainers say that tabbies and ginger cats are easiest to train, black cats the hardest and, unless the animal is neutered, there's no point in trying – they have more important things on their minds. In my experience cats are quite teachable, they quickly understand what is allowed and what is not but, unlike dogs, they have no vested interest in conforming to the house rules. Dogs, being pack animals, want to fit in and please the pack leader, their owner. A stern word can leave a well-trained dog cowed and sorrowful. A stern word to a cat will produce a cross, resentful look that says 'I can't think why you are being so horrid to me'. They have no interest in pleasing you, so they will only do what pleases

them most at the time. They are easily startled, so they can be trained to stop scratching your armchair or jumping onto the mantelpiece by a thrown newspaper or a loud noise, but they are very clever at identifying the times when unpleasant results will not be forthcoming. Their philosophy seems simple: 'You didn't see me, so I didn't do it.' My two six-year-old British Blues, Emma and Oliver, know that they are forbidden to touch the Christmas tree when it makes its annual appearance and they also know that for at least half an hour every morning, between being let out of the kitchen and welcoming the family down for breakfast, they have the unsupervised run of the house. When humans are about the cats ignore the tree completely; those swinging baubles and tinsel strands apparently hold not the slightest interest. But for each of the twelve days of Christmas we come down each morning to a trail of chewed crackers and sucked angels.

RIGHT: *Most cats will get used to a harness, if asked – but that doesn't mean they will enjoy the experience.*

RIGHT: *An odd-eyed white Persian. In white cats, blue eyes are often associated with deafness.*

CHAPTER TWO

Aristocratic Cats

The very first official cat show, held at London's Crystal Palace in 1871, was organized by artist and author Harrison Weir, who wanted the general public to appreciate the beauty of cats and pay more attention to careful breeding. Persians, Angoras and the newly imported Siamese were among those represented, though at the time there were no official pedigrees, as no one had thought of recording a cat's family tree. 170 cats were on display; so many people came to admire them that visitors complained that it was impossible to see the cats for the crowds, and a second show was arranged to cater for this enthusiastic interest a few months later.

Over the next few years the idea of cat shows took hold and in 1887 the world's first governing body for the cat world, the National Cat Club, was formed in the UK and began a register of pedigrees. Other clubs came and went, but in 1910 the major British cat clubs united to become the Governing Council of the Cat Fancy, which is still in being today.

Small shows had been held in various parts of the USA for some years before the first important event was organized in Madison Square Garden in 1895 by an Englishman, James Hyde. Interest in selective breeding grew quickly and the American Cat Club was set up in 1896 to keep a stud book and to arrange the sponsorship of shows. Now the USA has several registering bodies, the largest of them, the Cat Fanciers' Association, was established in 1906.

The new favourites

As owners became more conscious of the differences between breeds of cats and could see and compare them at exhibitions, the cats with long silky coats became the favourites, and when Queen Victoria acquired two blue Persians, their popularity was assured.

There is some argument about the origin of these cats but it seems likely that similar types evolved in the mountainous regions of Persia (now Iran), Turkey and China. In the early shows both Persians, the stockier cats with long, heavy coats, and Angoras, with silkier coats and smaller, less rounded heads, were well represented and the two types were bred together. Eventually the Persian strain predominated and until recently, when breeders became interested in re-establishing Angoras as a breed in their own right, they had almost disappeared.

Many Persians were exported to the USA in the 1900s and by the early part of this century had displaced the 'home-grown' longhair, the Maine Coon, in the championship stakes. In the USA they still keep the official title of Persian, but in Britain they are classified by the more prosaic name of 'Longhairs', with each colour given a breed number of its own.

Persians are calm, peaceful cats, loving towards their owners but content to be left alone during the working day. They are very handsome cats with broad heads, tiny ears and large round eyes. Their coats, long and flowing, stand away from their bodies and a full ruff frames their faces. Though they are undemanding by temperament, their coats need a great deal of attention. If they miss a day's grooming their coats are liable to develop tangles, and they moult all the time so their owners' chairs and clothes are always covered in hairs.

Over sixty colours are recognized in the United States and over thirty in the United Kingdom. Blues are the most popular in the UK, where they have entire shows to themselves. In the USA, where Blues have been losing out in popularity, Cream was recognized as a desirable colour from the beginning, though British breeders only became interested in the 1920s. Some of the most beautiful of Longhairs are the Chinchillas, their white coats tipped with black, brown or red, giving off a silvery sparkle.

FACING PAGE: *Persians are ideal indoor cats, being content to be left alone during the day.*

ABOVE: *Ragdolls are apparently comfortable in any position, their legs hanging down at all sorts of odd angles.*

Native Americans

The oldest native breed of Longhairs in the USA, the Maine Coon, won 'best in show' at Madison Square Garden in 1895 but when Persians became ultra-fashionable it was pushed into the background. It has only recently come back into popularity and was imported to England for the first time in the 1980s. The romantic story of the beginnings of the breed is that it descended from six Angoras belonging to the French queen Marie Antoinette. When the royal family planned to escape from France, the legend goes, they sent ahead their most treasured possessions, including their cats, to the *Sally*, a ship captained by a sailor from Maine. The king and queen were arrested and imprisoned before they could join the ship and there was nothing left for the captain to do but to sail for home. When the Angoras reached the USA, they mated with the local stock and their offspring developed the thick, shaggy coats needed to survive the New England winters. They were named 'coon' because their colouring and bushy tails reminded the people of racoons.

The first Maine Coons were mostly brown tabbies but now these large sturdy cats come in all colours. The coat is shorter on the shoulders. longer on the stomach and back legs, so that they seem to be wearing furry breeches. They are useful working cats and their sociable, intelligent characters also make them good pets but they are independent and like to roam free, so they are not well suited to an indoor life.

The Ragdolls, too, originated in the United States but much later, in the

1960s. The first litter resulted from a mating between Josephine, a white Angora-type cat and a Seal-point male called Daddy War Bucks, whose father was a Birman. Josephine had been injured in a road accident, which left her extremely placid and with a very high pain threshold, and she was supposed to have passed on these qualities to her kittens, which got their name from their habit of flopping limply in the arms of someone they trust. Most of the claims that have grown up around Ragdolls – that they do not feel pain, that they flop about because their skeleton differs from that of other cats and that they have no instinct for self-preservation – have been disproved by experts, but Ragdolls do seem to have particularly sweet natures and, unlike most cats, they like being cradled in the arms like babies. They will also throw themselves down to sleep in the most unlikely places, and will climb onto a lap at every opportunity, purring vigorously. They are such dependable purrers that a Ragdoll raised £200 for charity in a sponsored television 'Purrathon' by purring continuously for forty-three minutes.

Ragdolls are large, heavily built cats,

with an average male weighing 6.8-9 kg (15-20 lb) and have semi-long, silky coats in four colours: Seal, Blue, Lilac and Chocolate, though these cannot be distinguished easily until the kittens are several months old. They often follow their owner about with a dog-like devotion, come when they are called and even respond to a whistle. Their playful, good-natured dispositions mean that they blend easily into households with children and other pets.

ABOVE: *Two British Blues – a popular choice of colour with cat owners.*

25

The original cats

The British, European and American Shorthairs are the nearest breeds to the original domestic cats, their appearance little altered to suit breeding fashions. Their bodies are solid and powerful, their coats easy to manage and their health excellent. They appeared frequently at early shows and Harrison Weir, responsible for drawing up the first standards for pedigree cats, said that: 'A high-class short-haired cat is one of the most perfect animals ever created.' There is little difference between the British and the European Shorthairs with their large round eyes, dense plush coats and overall chunky look. They are intelligent and gentle, affectionate with their owners but unwilling to let strangers take liberties. Their ancestry makes them keen hunters.

Blue is probably the most popular colour in the UK, particularly over the past few years, since a brand of upmarket cat food began using British Blues in their advertisements, showing them

RIGHT: *Some catteries refuse to accept Siamese cats, because their noisy voices disturb the other residents.*

26

rubbing lovingly round their owner's face. the French have a Blue Shorthair called the Chartreux and there is controversy over whether these cats belong to the same breed as the British Blue or are a different variety. The Chartreux were reputedly bred by the Carthusian monks who began breeding with cats brought back by knights from the Crusades in a monastery near Grenoble, where they also produce their famous liqueur.

When the first settlers set out for the New World, they always took cats to keep down the rodents on board ship and protect their precious food supplies. On arrival, the cats mated with cats brought from other parts of the world, and when the first pedigree Shorthairs were registered, they were imported English cats. The first all-American Shorthair registered was Buster Brown in 1904. American Shorthairs are larger, leaner and more athletic than their British cousins with hardier coats, animals well suited for a hearty outdoor life. In the 1960s selective breeding produced the Exotic Shorthair, aiming to combine the good qualities of both Shorthairs and Persians. Exotics have the more rounded shape, cobby body and calm temperament of the Persian with the short, easy-care coat and alertness of the Shorthair. They were first recognized for showing in 1967.

The oriental touch

Legend says that a Princess of Siam used to slide her valuable rings onto her cat's tail at night, so that she knew where to find them in the morning but some of them slid off and rolled onto the floor, so she had to hunt for them. To keep them safe, she tied a knot in the cat's tail and that is how Siamese came by the kink in their tails – a kink which counts as a fault on the show bench. The breed is supposed to be about 400 years old, originating in Thailand, once called Siam, where they were kept by royalty and priests. They were sometimes presented as diplomatic gifts; the two shown at the Crystal Palace in 1885 were a gift from the King of Siam to the British Consul-General in Bangkok.

At first Siamese were quite solidly built cats with roundish faces but now they are slim and delicately boned with wedge-shaped heads. They still have a regal look about them with their bright blue almond-shaped eyes, large pointed ears

and sleek, shining coats. Their manner can be imperious; they demand attention, dislike being left alone and can be fiercely jealous of a new baby or another pet. They are quick to learn tricks and games and just as quick to learn how to open the refrigerator door and help themselves to a tasty snack. They have very distinctive voices and have no hesitation in using them, so they can be very noisy.

The Burmese is another elegant cat; its voice is reminiscent of the Siamese but much quieter and less often used. It is a sweet-natured and friendly cat – sometimes too friendly for its own good, as it is outgoing and trusting towards the whole world. It likes to share a bed with its owner and seem to be able to sense a human being's moods and respond to them.

The line of the Burmese can be traced back to Wong Mau, a cat who was imported into San Francisco in 1930 by a retired ship's doctor after a visit to Burma. Wong Mau was first mated to a Siamese but it was only when she was mated back to one of her own offspring that she produced brown kittens like herself. The Burmese was first introduced into the UK in 1948; there, the breed has developed with longer legs and a less rounded, more tapering face than the American variety.

Wong Mau was probably a Tonkinese – if anyone had known, at the time, that such a cat existed. The breed, as such, was developed by a Canadian breeder in the 1960s, mating Burmese and Siamese. The result is a Siamese looking cat with lovely aquamarine eyes, a mixture of the Siamese blue and the Burmese gold. Its character, too, is an interesting mix of both parents: it has the strong will and intelligence of the Siamese and the affectionate sweetness of the Burmese. When two 'Tonks' mate, about half of the kittens will be Tonkinese; the rest can be either Siamese or Burmese.

Another close relative of the Burmese is the striking Bombay, so called because it looks like an Indian black panther. It first appeared in the US, the result of a cross between a black American Shorthair and a brown Burmese. Its outstanding characteristic is its intense black coat which shines like patent leather. Bombays are good-tempered, active cats who love human company and could rival the Ragdolls in a purring competition.

Like the Siamese, the silver-blue Korat

with its green-gold eyes comes from Thailand. It is named after a province in its own country, where it is known as 'Si-Sawat', or 'good fortune.' It was always quite a rare animal, and a wedding gift of a pair of these cats was thought to ensure a lifetime of good luck for the bridal couple. The Korat's heart-shaped face, sweet expression, glowing eyes and affectionate, fun-loving nature make it a particularly appealing pet for someone who is at home most of the time. It dislikes loud noises and extremes of temperature, so it will happily stay indoors but will not be happy if it is left alone too much.

The first Korats to arrive in the USA were litter mates Nara and Darra, a gift for an Oregon woman who had spent some time in Thailand. It was first accepted for championship competition in 1966 and breeders have worked hard to preserve its original looks.

The extroverts

Abyssinians look like wild cats but they like to be part of the family, though they tend to attach themselves to one person. They are fun-loving, outgoing cats who need their freedom; they do not take well

ABOVE: *Burmese cats tend to be outgoing and trusting towards the whole world.*

29

to being confined and are definitely not cats for apartment living. They are slender and lithe, with long, elegant necks, expressive eyes and small oval paws, so that they seem to be walking on tiptoe. They are often called 'bunny cats' because each hair of the coat is 'ticked' – banded with colour – like that of the rabbit, though the rabbit's fur has only one band of colour, while the cat has two or three. Originally, Abyssinians were all one colour, a reddish brown ticked with black, but now they can be 'Sorrel' (deep copper red ticked with brown) 'Blue' (blue-grey ticked with darker blue), Fawn, Lilac or Cream.

According to legend the Abyssinian, as well as the Egyptian Mau, is directly descended from the sacred cats of Egypt. Breed records show that the founder of the breed was Zula, a cat brought from Abyssinia (now Ethiopia) in 1868 by Captain Barrett Lennard following a British military expedition. They have never been easy to breed, as the females tend to produce small litters at lengthy intervals. The Second World War decimated the breeding programme in Britain, so that only a handful of pedigree animals remained after the war but by then the

breed, which had been founded by the arrival of two cats called Aluminium and Salt in the early years of the century, was well established in the USA.

The Rex cats had more homely beginnings. In 1950 a Cornish farm cat called Serena took a fancy to a passing tom and produced a litter of kittens. Four of them were just as expected but the fifth, called Kallibunker, had a curly coat. Experimental breeding produced more curly coats and the cats were called Cornish Rex because Rex rabbits have a similar curl. The first Devon Rex, Kirlee, appeared in 1960, when his mother, a stray, gave birth to a litter in the shelter of a hedge. This Rex turned out to be the product of different genes from the Cornish Rex and, after an inauspicious start in life, Kirlee went on to found a dynasty. Several Rexes went to the USA early on, both from England and from Germany, where a Rex had appeared shortly after Kallibunker's birth.

Both Cornish and Devon Rex cats have slim, elegant bodies. The coat of the Cornish Rex is thick and plush, while that of the Devon Rex is shorter and coarser, but they both feel surprisingly warm to the touch. The Devon Rex gets its distinctive

RIGHT: *A sorrel Abyssinian cat watches over her two-week-old kitten as it explores its home.*

look from a little pixie-like face topped with huge, bat ears. Owners who are allergic to cat fur can often keep a Rex without discomfort.

Rexes need little grooming but plenty of warmth – and lots and lots of attention. They don't like to be left alone for long and often prefer human friends to other animals. In spite of their delicate looks they are quite tough and full of fun and energy, always finding some new mischief to keep them interested.

Show cats

In the early days of cat shows, before inoculations were available, infection could spread like wildfire and sometimes whole catteries, with their carefully selected breeding stock, were wiped out within days, so that some owners were convinced that their cats had been poisoned by a rival at the show. Now cats can be protected against infection by regular injections, but shows are still risky places for pedigree cats. Cats will normally make their debut at small local shows before they move on to major events, so that they get used to being penned and handled by strangers. They must also learn to

tolerate a great deal of careful grooming, as their colour, coat and other characteristics must be displayed to perfection. Shorthairs escape comparatively lightly with brushing and combing followed by a polish with a chamois leather, but Longhairs will need lengthy daily combing and probably a bath two or three days before a show. Few cats like water and though pedigree stars become accustomed to a regular bath, they usually manage to look thoroughly affronted throughout the process.

Each country has its own governing body, or bodies; standards for breeds, as well as the names of breeds, can vary from one to another. The style of shows varies, too. In north America and most of Europe, the main hall is a colourful display of decorated cat pens with curtains and carpets and even rocking cradles or four-poster beds for their occupants. The outside of the pen is often festooned with rosettes, ribbons and photographs showing former triumphs or the cat's regal ancestry. When their class is called, the cats are taken into another room, or judging 'ring', where they are housed in identical pens and taken out, one by one, for assessment. In the UK, Australia and

New Zealand, the judges go to the cats, rather than the other way round, so the pens are kept completely anonymous and the only furniture allowed is a white blanket, white litter tray and feeding dishes. The judges bring a mobile table to each pen in turn.

Few cats actively enjoy shows, unlike dogs who have fun showing off and meeting other dogs. For a cat, it means being penned up for hours on end, then hauled out and prodded by strangers. Most put up with it but a few really hate it and spend the day with their heads under the blanket, pretending none of it is happening. Owners sometimes have to remove a panicky cat from the show scene altogether, as an animal that spends all its time struggling frantically with the judges is unlikely to win many prizes, though some very nervous cats seem to come into their own at a show, preening themselves proudly on the judging table.

LEFT: *Devon Rex cats are full of energy, and are not nearly as fragile as their looks suggest.*

CHAPTER THREE

An Elegant Creature

The cat's body has remained as nature intended. Whatever the breed, the basic structure is the same, unlike dogs, which have been specially bred for various tasks: retrieving, guarding, burrowing and so on. The cat began as a hunter and a killer, and so it has remained, even though it may live a cosseted lifestyle with all meals provided. Its acute senses enable it to locate its prey and, once the hunt is under way, it is capable of short bursts of speed and athletic leaps and bounds. Staying power is not necessary for the feline hunter; agility and stealth are essential. Its claws are designed for catching and gripping and its mouth is just the right size to fasten round the neck of its natural prey and deliver the killing bite.

The cat expends the minimum of energy in walking, conserving all its strength for hunting. The hindquarters are heavily muscled for acceleration and powerful leaps. The vertebrae are less tightly connected than those in the human body so that the cat can arch its back and twist and turn, and the narrow chest, lacking any true collarbone, enables it to squeeze through narrow spaces.

Seeing

Cats have large eyes set well forward in the head; the two fields of vision overlap to give a good stereoscopic effect, though when a cat is about to pounce it will sway its head from side to side to make the most accurate assessment of positioning and distance. Its eyesight is most accurate

FACING PAGE: *Cats walk silently on tiptoe, the thick pads on their feet acting as brakes and shock absorbers.*

LEFT: *The cat's acute eyesight and hearing are designed for use in hunting and self-preservation.*

ABOVE: *A cat's ears can pick up the smallest noise and pinpoint its direction precisely.*

by layers of highly reflective cells called the *tapetum lucidum* or 'bright carpet', which act as a mirror, reflecting the light forward. This is what causes the cat's eyes to glow green-gold (or red in the case of blue eyes) when caught by artificial light. In daytime, the delicate structure of the cat's eyes needs protection from strong light, and the pupils adjust to varying light by narrowing or dilating.

At one time, scientists thought that cats were colour-blind and could see only shades of grey but they have now demonstrated that they can distinguish colours – red from blue or green and blue from green, for instance – but this takes quite a lot of training, so it seems likely that they don't see them very clearly and that colours are certainly not important in their perceptions.

Hearing

Cats have such sensitive hearing that loud noises upset them. They can differentiate accurately between a wide range of sounds; pet cats will hear the slightest chink of their food bowls from the other end of the house and distinguish it from all the other crockery. The cone-shaped

at a good hunting distance of 2-6 m (7-20 ft); nearer than that and it sees best when an object is moving. I once watched a cat chasing a gecko across a wall in Jerusalem, patting playfully at its tail.

It is at night that a cat's eyes really come into their own. Though it cannot see in total darkness, the cat needs only a fraction of the light necessary for human vision. The back of the retina is covered

outer ear has more than a dozen muscles, enabling it to move forwards, sideways and backwards to catch the slightest sound. Cats can hear two octaves higher than humans – an essential ability when their prey emits high-pitched squeaks. Hearing seems to remain acute even when a cat is sleeping, for at the slightest rustle or the distant chirp of a bird, the cat will be wide awake and ready for action in an instant.

Smelling and tasting

The sense of smell is extremely important to the cat. Its nasal membrane has about 20 million nerve endings, four times the number in the human nose, and sniffing and smelling give it essential information about food, territory and mating. Cats identify one another by sniffing and, if you have mixed with other cats while you are out visiting, your pet will want to check you out very carefully to learn all about them. If one cat from a family goes to be mated, she will come back smelling of the unknown stud and the other cats may well reject her. The same may happen to an owner who puts on an unfamiliar perfume.

Some smells are obviously more interesting than others and most cats are sent into ecstasies by the herb catnip (*Nepeta cataria*). Some experts suggest that catnip gives off a smell like that from a substance excreted by a female on heat but, whatever the reason, it gives cats a 'high' as they roll in it, rub their faces in it and drift into a happy trance. I recently bought a new toy, impregnated with catnip, for my own cats. It was sealed in a cellophane packet, inside a paper bag with the top folded twice. I left it on the table while I unpacked my shopping and by the time I turned round Oliver had torn open the paper bag, demolished the cellophane packet and was clutching the toy to his chest, his eyes rolled upwards in sheer bliss.

Taste and smell are very closely associated. Cats will always test their food, by sniffing before they eat, often rejecting anything unfamiliar without trying it. Some cats do develop a taste for unlikely foods, such as olives, corn on the cob or puffed wheat; Ernest Hemingway's cat had a preference for mangoes and avocados. Unlike dogs they do not have a 'sweet tooth' and it is often said that they have no ability to taste sweet things, but I

FACING PAGE: If a cat's sense of smell is blocked for any reason, it may go off its food because it cannot test it by sniffing.

38

ABOVE: *The cat does not have a true collarbone, allowing it to squeeze through very narrow spaces.*

remember one cat who was perfectly trustworthy when left with the Sunday joint but would turn thief and scavenge for sugary doughnuts, attacking cake boxes and raiding visitors' plates.

Teeth and eating

Cats are carnivores, equipped with teeth ideal for killing and devouring their prey. The four large canines deliver the killing bite, then the molars shear the flesh. None of the cat's teeth are adapted to chewing, for its method of eating is to tear pieces from its prey and swallow them whole. A mouse is eaten head first, bones and all; likewise small birds, though the wing and tail feathers may be discarded. When dealing with larger birds, the cat will usually pluck them first, pulling out feathers with its teeth and spitting them out. The cat's digestive juices are far stronger than ours and are capable of breaking down bone, though fur and feathers are often regurgitated.

Fur and whiskers

One of the great pleasures of stroking a cat is the feel of its silky or velvety fur, but

to the cat, its coat is important for protection and insulation. A cat's coat is made up of guard hairs which form the outer coat and a layer of more bristly awn hairs, both of which act as protection from the elements and from injury to the skin. Below them are the fluffy down hairs that keep the animal warm, though not all breeds have all three types of hair. The coat forms a good insulating blanket but the cat can turn down the heat in warm weather by washing itself.

A fine set of whiskers is a handsome sight, but their purpose is not decorative. They are extremely sensitive to touch and the cat uses them to test out the environment. They are width gauges to signal to the cat that its body can squeeze through a narrow space and navigational aids in the dark, when they can sense the minute air currents given off by solid objects, so that the cat can feel its way about without colliding with obstacles. If a cat's whiskers are damaged, its ability to hunt suffers badly.

Climbing and jumping

Cats are natural high-wire artists, picking their way daintily along the top of a fence or balancing on a gatepost. They can also make accurate jumps of five times their height from a crouching start, leaving enough clearance for their hind legs to get a steady hold. However, when your cat makes a nonchalant leap from the bed to the wardrobe, only pausing long enough to tense its body, it is acting from memory. The height, the landing place and the amount of push needed from the hindquarters have been tested, so the cat knows exactly what it is doing.

In the case of a new jump it would take its time to measure and plan before launching off. The day after we had changed our kitchen cabinets, Emma sprang up to her favourite sleeping place on top of the wall cabinet only to fail miserably and come crashing down onto the work surface, looking very ruffled and resentful. Once she had done some hard grooming to regain her dignity, she eyed the distance carefully, swaying her head from side to side for extra accuracy, gathered herself together and leapt again, this

RIGHT: *Cats are natural high-wire artists, having no fear of heights and an impeccable sense of balance.*

41

time making a perfect landing. When a cat is jumping downwards it is more cautious for it has to land on its weaker front legs; it edges forwards, hanging over the edge as far as possible to shorten the distance, then thrusts off with its hind legs.

A climbing cat is a pleasure to watch: a tree climb usually begins with a leap, then the cat stretches out a paw at a time, grips with its claws and pulls itself upwards, its hindquarters helping with propulsion. Coming down is a different story altogether, and probably the only ungainly type of movement that the cat makes. Its claws curve the wrong way for descending, and its powerful hindquarters can be little help, so it usually comes down backwards, clinging on grimly and shifting in small, tentative steps until it is low enough to jump, twisting its body so that it lands on all fours. The difficulty of coming down backwards is the reason that cats often get stuck in trees: in the excitement of the moment they run up too far, then baulk at the fearful descent.

LEFT: *Some cats may stay at the top of trees for days rather than attempt the descent.*

Of course, cats have the reputation for always landing on their feet. This is due to a special sense organ in the inner ear which can tell the brain the exact position of the head and its rate of movement and the moment the cat falls the 'self-righting reflex' comes automatically into play and a series of twists of the body enable the cat to position itself for a safe landing. A New York survey found that 90 per cent of cats falling from city skyscrapers survived, though many suffered broken legs or pelvises. Those falling over 26 m (85 ft) did best, probably because they had more time to complete all their self-righting movements and they could relax their bodies ready for a softer landing.

Extra senses

Extrasensory perception among cats has been debated for many years. Every earthquake or volcanic eruption brings new stories of a mother cat who carried her kittens to safety several hours before the disaster struck, or a strange exodus of cats from a doomed village twenty-four hours beforehand. These cats are feeling and hearing changes that are imperceptible to us, detecting the minute earth tremors and changes in electrostatic activity which precede any such violent event, in the same way that we sometimes get headaches when a thunderstorm is on the way. When your cat, snoozing on your lap, suddenly sits bolt upright, staring at some empty corner of the room, it has probably spotted some tiny particle of fluff stirred by an air current or has heard a faint movement from the other side of the wall.

In the bombing of Britain during the Second World War some cat owners found that their cats gave warning when a bombing raid was on the way; as soon as they saw the cat taking refuge in the safest place in the house, usually under the stairs, they knew it was time to take to the shelter.

These cats were able to hear and identify the bombers several minutes before they were audible to humans – one owner reckoned that his cat could hear them 80 km (50 miles) away – just the way a cat knows when its special human is on the way home because it has heard the distinctive note of the car engine in the far distance. When it runs to the door in greeting, it is demonstrating its ultra sharp senses, not its psychic powers.

CHAPTER FOUR

Family Cat

When a female is ready for mating, she will leave you in little doubt. First comes the rolling and rubbing, an urgent seeking of affection, punctuated by restless pacing, then the 'calling', a polite name for the yowling and wailing by which she signals to possible mates. Her rolling takes on a look of desperation, she will try to escape at the slightest opportunity and all the toms of the neighbourhood will gather hopefully at your door. The breeding season will vary according to the climate of the country in which the cat lives, with a break so that the kittens do not arrive in the coldest weather. Some cats, living a warm indoor life, carry on the oestrus cycles for most of the year.

When the female is taken to stud she will mate with the chosen tom a number of times over several days but the mating does not invariably 'take' and if it is unsuccessful, she will come back into oestrus quite soon. If she is pregnant, the first sign will probably be an increase in appetite, but her abdomen will only show swelling after about five weeks. The mother-to-be takes better care of herself, taking plenty of rest, washing herself meticulously and, as she grows bigger, instinctively avoiding jumping too high or squeezing through narrow gaps. Pregnancy lasts about nine weeks, and only the cat will know exactly when her litter is due. Near the time she will start searching for a suitable nest, probably ignoring the hygienic and suitable arrangements made by her owner. A door left open by mistake can mean she is busily shredding

FACING PAGE: *On the whole, cats are attentive and affectionate mothers, taking meticulous care of their litter.*

45

ABOVE: *Two seven-day-old kittens curl up together for a nap.*

until too late. The baby had to make do with being carried round in a sling for several weeks.

New arrivals

Once the cat goes into labour she will pace restlessly and refuse food; after a few hours, when the second, short, stage of labour begins, she will retire to her nest. Then the first kitten starts to emerge. The birth of each kitten involves the same stages of labour but the gap between their arrival can be a few minutes or several hours. Unless anything goes wrong, and human intervention is needed, the mother cat will look after the whole business of labour and its aftermath, acting on instinct, and she may purr from beginning to end. When all the kittens have arrived she will wash her tail end then curl round them so that they can suckle.

The new born kittens are very fragile, weighing only about 113 g (4 oz); they cannot see, hear or stand and are completely dependent on their mother. Most cats make very good mothers and care for their litter selflessly but there are exceptions. I know one British Shorthair, with a

the newspapers under the sink, scratching at the towels in the cupboard or even cuddling up to the shoes in your wardrobe. One imperious female called Clarissa, who always knew on which side her bread was buttered, bedded down in the baby's pram and was not discovered

splendid pedigree, who was bought by a breeder hoping to produce future show champions, only to find that Victoria refused to have anything to do with her kittens. The moment she was able, she walked away from them and from then on, even if she was shut in a room with them, she refused them her milk. A mother with a litter seems well disposed towards all helpless infants and will usually accept an abandoned or orphaned kitten but if no handy foster-mother is available, such a kitten can be successfully reared by hand, with bottle feeds every two hours. Kittens 'fostered' by humans often grow up to be particularly affectionate but they are vulnerable in the early stages because they lack the colostrum contained in their mother's milk, which provides immunity from disease.

First steps

In the kittens' first week, every meal is important, as they will double their body

RIGHT: *Feline mothers may be so devoted that they will not leave their litter for a moment.*

LEFT: *Cream and blue kittens at six weeks, with their lilac-tortoiseshell mother.*

FACING PAGE: *A tortoiseshell cat retrieves her ginger kitten, holding it gently but firmly by the scruff of the neck.*

weight in this time. By the time they are ten days old, often sooner, their eyes will be open, though it will be another week before they are functioning properly. Their hearing, too, develops gradually in sensitivity. Though the sense of smell is present from birth, this also will be refined and intensified over the coming months. After a fortnight or so, they will begin to crawl about on their tummies, and in another week they will start walking on wobbly legs. Once they are able to explore, their mother will keep a close eye on them, rounding them up and chivvying them back into the nest if they are straying too far.

Some time within the first few weeks, the mother cat will probably change to a new nesting site, carrying the kittens one at a time, holding them by the scruff of the neck. This seems to be a throw-back to wild cat behaviour, when the first nest would be chosen for its safe position and the second for its closeness to good hunting grounds. Though domestic cats have no need to hunt for their food, the instinct seems to be too strong to resist. Unfortunately, cats often seem to desert a comfortable, well-placed nest for somewhere both unsuitable and inconvenient.

49

I remember one owner who left a door unlatched by mistake when she left for work and came back to find the whole litter ensconced in her food cupboard. One kitten was picking its way gingerly across the tops of a dozen eggs, another was snuggled up to a lettuce and the third was trying to pry the plastic wrap from a trifle. The mother was spread regally across the baked bean cans, with every air of a job well done.

The kittens take a first step towards independence when weaning begins with milky cereal feeds or pureed baby food at about three weeks. Soon after, as the first teeth come through, they can manage their first feeds of minced meat. By the end of the second month, they are playing together energetically. In their play they rehearse the skills an independent cat would need in later life; in crouching to pounce on a waving tail, stalking a playmate or jumping out on an unsuspecting playmate from the cover of a chair leg they are mimicking adult hunting behaviour and when they roll over together, kicking and punching, or fluff their fur in mock anger, to look as big and menacing as possible, they are learning to defend themselves. In the wild, cats leave this play behaviour behind as soon as they tackle the serious business of life, but pet cats will keep it up all their lives, as an outlet for their energies and a way of bonding with their owners.

The mother cat plays a vital role in training her offspring, communicating with them with a range of different sounds, according to whether she wants to soothe and comfort, chasten or admonish or greet and welcome and an owner can learn to distinguish the sounds quite easily. If the mother has access to a litter tray, she will deal with any necessary toilet training, growling or prodding her infants until they get the idea. If she is allowed out of doors she will begin to instruct them in hunting, first bringing home dead prey, which well-fed kittens will treat like a toy mouse, and later live creatures, so that they begin practising catching, holding and perhaps even killing, in earnest.

At eight weeks or so, when the kittens are fully weaned, they are ready to leave their mother but, of course, no one has told them about this, and they find it all very bewildering. They are not capable of looking ahead and don't think beyond their next meal but suddenly they are

FACING PAGE: *Two ginger kittens mock-fighting, practising skills they may use later in life.*

taken away from everything they know, with not even a familiar smell to reassure them. All the same, because kittens are naturally friendly and curious, they cope remarkably well. Reactions vary, of course: your kitten may pop out of the carrier, have a quick sniff round and look up at you with a face that says: 'This looks a good place, how about a game?' or it may need to check out every corner, to make sure there are no bogeymen lurking before it stops glowering in suspicion.

Some surprises

The first few days can bring surprises for the new owner, too. Kittens are very small and supple and can squeeze into unbelievably tiny spaces. Many a new arrival has been found climbing around the back of the refrigerator or crouching under the cooker.

Kittens are adventurous and fearless, as unconscious of hazards as a toddler, as they poke their noses into rubbish bins (chicken bones, sharp tins, polythene bags), sewing boxes (pins, needles, buttons) and kitchen cupboards (all sorts of toxic chemicals). If they are too quiet, they may well have settled down in a corner to chew on the electric wires and though they might not yet have the power in their hindquarters to jump onto a stove full of boiling pans, it won't be long! All the time they are testing their climbing skills and are quite likely to freeze in fright halfway up a tree or misjudge a jump and find themselves hanging from a ledge by their front paws, unsure of their ability to make the drop and hoping for rescue.

Kittens are just as individual as people. You may acquire two kittens that look like identical twins; at first they sleep, demand food and become active at exactly the same time, as if programmed by an invisible clock. Very soon, however, their own personalities will show through. One will peer suspiciously at visitors from beneath the sofa while the other gambols happily out to meet them; one has a purr like an engine on full throttle while the other manages a few rusty grunts in moments of extreme ecstasy; one is fastidious to the point of obsession while the other is a natural slob. The cat owners who add yet another member to their feline family every few months do so because they just can't resist the lure of yet another unique little personality.

ABOVE: *Sharing a bowl of milk. Kittens are fully weaned and ready to leave their mother at about eight weeks.*

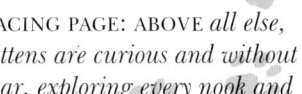

FACING PAGE: ABOVE *all else, kittens are curious and without fear, exploring every nook and cranny of their new world.*

CHAPTER FIVE

A Cat's Day

A good day, in cat's terms, probably includes several hours of sleeping and napping, plenty of opportunity to watch the world go by, a few games and cuddles with the family, plus a little hunting and regular territorial checks, though indoor cats have to forego these and depend more on their human friends for entertainment.

Cats usually adapt to their owner's normal lifestyle and at the time when their wild relatives would be hunting for food, our well-fed pets go to bed by our clocks, though they will usually prowl about for some time after the humans have retired, gazing out into the night, where they seem to find all manner of interesting things to watch. They rise, naturally enough, with the birds and if you let your cat sleep in the bedroom you are probably used to a furry bundle landing on your chest at about 5 a.m., purring encouragingly into your face. I know one cat who learned that he could rouse the whole family if he turned on the teenage son's ghetto-blaster. He did it by accident one morning, stepping on the 'play' button with a heavy paw, and was rewarded by a flurry of footsteps and an early plate of food. After that, unless his owner remembered to hide away the radio last thing at night, early mornings were the norm.

Cosy cat

The cat spends two-thirds of its life sleeping. Most of the time it has the knack of

55

LEFT: *Cats will find their own entrances and exits, often scorning specially installed cat flaps.*

FACING PAGE: *Cats are fastidious about keeping themselves clean and tidy; it is rare to see a healthy cat looking bedraggled.*

searching out comfortable places, choosing warm, soft fabrics rather than chilly, slippery ones but occasionally it will choose a most inhospitable perch to take a snooze – in the middle of coils of electrical flex, on the top of a pile of books or balanced on a narrow fence. Mostly it is only 'cat-napping'; for only about a third of its total sleeping time, for short periods of a few minutes at a stretch, does the cat sleep deeply. During deep sleep cats dream, perhaps reliving the thrill of the chase, and their paws and whiskers twitch, their ears flick backwards and forwards and they may make little mewing or purring noises.

Before settling down for a sleep, a cat will often circle round several times, making the instinctive movements of settling into the nest. Once the settling process is over it may stretch out, if it is warm (particularly in the direct heat of the fire) and completely at ease, or it may curl into a ball if it wants to warm up. The nose is the most cold-sensitive part of its body and on chilly days the cat will use its tail as a portable blanket, wrapping it around its face. Sometimes a cat will lay its paw across its nose to cut the flow of oxygen and help send it to sleep. Cats love heat and will wrap themselves round the fire grate or lean against the radiator without any apparent discomfort: in fact, they have far more tolerance of heat than humans and will only begin to feel pain at about 52°C (126°F). Many owners have been alerted to danger by the smell of singeing cat fur while their pets were still snoozing peacefully.

On waking, the cat may decide that a good wash is in order. The rough projections on the tongue, called papillae, which enable the hunter cat to scrape flesh from the bones of larger prey, also serve as a handy brush and comb. Friendly cats often groom one another, while regular grooming by the owner helps to cement the bond between cat and human: not only is the rhythmic brushing or combing pleasurable in itself, but the cat loves the feeling of being the centre of attention.

ABOVE: *A Siamese cat marks its territory by rubbing its scent glands against walls and doorways.*

The big world

The most docile, affectionate cat becomes a different animal once it emerges into the outside world. Then the jungle calls and the gentle, sleepy family pet can be instantly transformed into the scourge of the bird population, the prowling terror of the neighbourhood. In the wild, it would be essential to the cat's survival to establish territory and drive away all interlopers to preserve its supply of food.

Domestic cats have no such need but each will still mark out and defend its own patch. The size of the territory will vary according to circumstances: a country cat may control vast tracts of land while a town cat has only a small back yard for its domain. Indoor cats do not lose their territorial instinct and though they may never have to go into battle, they can be thrown into a frenzy if a strange cat wanders past the window or cries at the door.

A cat will patrol its territory regularly, usually taking exactly the same route, marking out the boundaries with its scent. It will rub its face against trees, walls or fences, often rearing on its hind legs to rub harder, then turn and rub with its tail end. A tom cat (and sometimes a neuter or female) will spray the bushes and other markers for good measure, backing up to the object, its tail high and quivering. Any visiting cat will know how recently the controller of this territory has re-asserted its claim, and that it trespasses at its peril. Within the territory, the cat will have several favourite spots for snoozing and surveying the world and will probably move around from one to the other at certain times of day.

Cats holding neighbouring territories

RIGHT: *To intimidate its enemies, a cornered cat will arch its back and stand stiff-legged to appear larger.*

will usually avoid one another but where there is a confrontation they will attempt to intimidate one another, circling each other on stiff legs, their heads tilted sideways as they glare fixedly, and yowl menacingly. In most cases, one or other will back down and slink away.

There is often common ground between neighbouring territories, a 'no-man's-land' used by all the cats, for even aggressive felines are capable of cooperation when it suits them. At one time we lived between two cats who were bitter rivals. William and Snoopy were both elderly males with no desire for all-out battle but they were both determined to maintain their status and the result was many a noisy stand-off. Their owners were out at work all day so both cats visited us frequently and there was much angry hissing and tail swishing if one caught us petting the other. Then one cold day with sheeting rain, first Snoopy and then William took refuge in my kitchen. Their eyes met and I saw them decide, in a split second, where their best interests lay. Slowly and stiffly, each cat turned its back. They spent the rest of the afternoon at opposite ends of the kitchen, studiously avoiding one another. The next day it was back to the usual yowling and prowling.

The mighty hunter

Two good meals a day, even with a few snacks in between, will not rid your cat of its hunting instinct. An indoor cat, watching a bird on a tree, will automatically switch into hunting mode, crouching down, swishing its tail in excited expectation, gathering its haunches ready to spring. Its teeth will chatter gently, perhaps in anticipation of clamping its jaws round a juicy morsel of prey – and the fact that it never has the opportunity to catch anything never seems to discourage or deter. It's no coincidence that these cats are eager for games that involve chasing, pouncing and leaping.

Outside, the cat will have its favourite spots for hunting and it will wait and watch for a suitable quarry with inexhaustible patience. When it has a bird in its sights, it drops down close to the ground and creeps along to close the gap. Once within striking distance it will gather itself ready for the pounce. A good pounce will pin down the prey ready for the kill though when domestic cats make

FACING PAGE: *Nothing, not even regular gourmet meals, will deter your cat from hunting.*

60

a catch, they often seem uncertain what to do with it. A wild cat would immediately kill and eat the animal in its grasp, but domestic cats will often prefer to prolong the chase by releasing the prey then pouncing again. Even if they do get round to the killing bite, they seldom eat their catch.

Routine matters

Several times a day a cat will feel the need for a session of vigorous stropping. Scratching is another of its inbuilt instincts and fulfils several purposes. It gets rid of the blunt outer layer of the claws so that the new sharp tips emerge; it is also a useful form of exercise. Cats also scratch convenient marking spots around their territory, leaving scent from the sweat on their paws. This sign of 'ownership' may be the reason that a cat will scratch at your favourite armchair, which smells strongly of you. There is also a form of greeting that involves hooking both sets of front claws into the side of your chair and stretching. It may not be good for your furniture but it obviously makes the cat feel happy!

Routine is very important to a cat: it gets safety and security from the fact that meals, playtimes, and quiet times always happen at the same time. A cat used to an evening play session will gaze at you in lazy wonderment and probably yawn disdainfully if you start dangling a ball on a string before its nose at afternoon nap time. Cats have a very efficient built-in time mechanism and if your pet is always found sitting on the hall table awaiting

ABOVE: *Your cat will know exactly when playtime is, and will expect you to adhere to the schedule.*

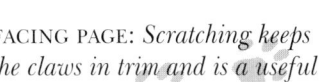

FACING PAGE: *Scratching keeps the claws in trim and is a useful form of exercise.*

your return from work, the chances are that, when you have a day off, it will be sitting in the same place at the usual time, ready for a few ecstatic head-butts.

All sorts of rituals surround food. One cat of my acquaintance will not eat unless he sees the food taken from the tin; meals served behind his back are unacceptable. Another knows that Thursday night is meat shopping night and vigorously demands her dollop of fresh mince, which must be eaten straight from the floor. Presumably she had her first taste of fresh mince from the kitchen floor, but no one remembers this but the cat.

The cat's instincts tell it that it needs to nibble grass as an extra to its home diet and this gives it a useful supplement of folic acid. It also gives it roughage and helps it to get rid of fur balls, which might otherwise cause an obstruction. Owners don't always appreciate the benefits of fresh grass when the cat comes straight back indoors to vomit on the carpet.

Cats and cream have always been linked in popular thinking but in fact many cats cannot digest cow's milk, let alone cream. Their natural drink is water, though some drink very little and they

LEFT: *Cats may nibble leaves on indoor or outdoor plants, so it is wise to avoid growing toxic plants around your home.*

very often scorn the clean bowl of water thoughtfully provided by their owners and choose to lap at puddles, ponds or even a birdbath, perhaps because the smell is more inviting than our chemically treated water. On the other hand, some cats prefer to drink from a dripping tap. This may be because, in the wild, it is safer to drink running rather than standing water – just one more reminder of the cat's savage ancestry.

RIGHT: *Most cats will keep away from large areas of water, but may approach the edge of a pond for a drink.*

CHAPTER SIX

Cats' Tales

There is a legend that, at the time of creation, all the animals were lined up so that each, in turn, could ask God for the attribute it most wanted. The peacock wanted beauty, the gazelle swiftness, the lion courage, the horse grace, and so on. The cat, last in line, listened to all the requests and, when its turn came, it asked for a little of everything – which is why the cat turned out to be the most perfect of animals.

Certainly the cat has, from the earliest times of its domestication, been regarded as a very special creature. In ancient Egypt the cat was revered for its association with the goddess Bastet, the bringer of good fortune for households which paid her homage. Bastet was sometimes portrayed with the head of a lioness, sometimes with that of a cat; she frequently had kittens at her feet or in a basket carried over her arm. She was both a sun and moon goddess; believers thought that the cat's eyes absorbed the rays of the sun during the day and reflected them back at night, thus ensuring that the sun would rise next morning.

Pampered pets

Pet cats wore jewelled collars or gold and silver chains around their necks and when they died the whole family went into mourning, wailing and shaving their eyebrows. The cat's remains would be mummified and, if their owners were rich, placed in mummy cases adorned with gold and jewels. They were then

FACING PAGE: Cats have an air of mystery that has led people to associate them with all sorts of magical powers.

67

buried in special cat cemeteries: in one of these, at Beni Hassan in central Egypt, over 300,000 feline mummies were unearthed. Killing a cat was forbidden on pain of death and one unfortunate soldier, who accidentally rode over a cat, was torn to pieces 'by the infuriated populace of Thebes'. In the fifth century BC, when the Persian army attacked Egypt, the invading forces used the veneration of cats to good effect: each soldier carried a cat on his shield, knowing that the Egyptian forces would not risk harming the sacred animal.

Today, the Egyptian Mau (mau is simply the word for cat), is said to be the direct descendant of the cats of ancient times. The Mau owes its modern type to the efforts of a Russian princess who took her spotted silver female Baba, descended from Egyptian stock, and two of Baba's offspring to the USA in 1956 but it was not until 1977 that the Cat Fanciers' Club granted championship status to this distinctive breed.

It seems likely that the early domestic cats were descended from the African wild cat. These creatures, larger than our domestic cats, were probably tempted into villages by the rodents raiding the grain stores. The early farmers, who relied on their harvests for survival, would have appreciated their usefulness and encouraged them, so that the cats were soon providing a regular mouse patrol in exchange for the warmth of the fire and some extra titbits.

Cats of Rome

In Egyptian tomb paintings cats are often shown sitting under a woman's chair, as a fertility symbol and one is depicted walking sedately on a leash. These cats always had faint tabby markings; it was not until they reached Europe and interbred with the fiercer, less easily domesticated European wild cats, that the stronger tabby markings that we recognize began to emerge. Though for centuries the Egyptians strictly forbade the export of their sacred animals, all this changed after 30 BC, when Egypt became a Roman province and cats were smuggled out of the country by Roman soldiers on their return home. It was probably the Romans who brought the first domesticated cats to Europe and cat remains have been found at many excavations of the period.

Though cats were no longer sacred

FACING PAGE: *The Egyptian Mau is said to be the direct descendant of the cats worshipped in ancient Egypt.*

ABOVE: *Cats have been the favoured companions of many world leaders, including the English king Charles I and US President Calvin Coolidge.*

they retained their air of mystery and other-worldliness and, in the Middle Ages, this was their downfall. Their historical link with pagan ceremonies was bad enough but at a time when superstition was rife, the unblinking stare of the cat was enough to confirm the belief that it could put a spell on an enemy and a cat's eyes shining in the dark were sure proof of demoniac possession.

At the height of the witch-hunts, having a cat walk through the door was enough to lead to the trial of poor old women for witchcraft. Witches were supposed to keep cats as their familiars and suckle them from an extra nipple, or even to take the guise of cats as they roamed the countryside, laying curses, causing cattle to die or casting the evil eye.

Rightful place

Cats were burned and tortured on a massive scale throughout Europe and not until the seventeenth century that they were restored to their rightful place in people's homes and affections. The English king Charles I kept a black cat which went everywhere with him. When it died he lamented 'my luck is gone' and he was absolutely right, for the next day he found himself under arrest and was later executed, on the orders of Oliver Cromwell. Dr Samuel Johnson, of dictionary fame, had a cat called Hodge, and used to make special trips to buy him oysters. He didn't like to send the servants out on these errands in case they came to resent the cat. US President Calvin Coolidge had a cat called Timmie, and his canary, Caruso, rode around on Timmie's back and snuggled down to sleep between his front paws. Slippers, Theodore Roosevelt's cat, also had an honoured place at the White House. When Slippers decided to stretch out across the path of a formal procession into a state banquet, Roosevelt led the whole line of dignitaries in a wide arc round the recumbent cat, rather than disturb his slumbers.

Mademoiselle Dupuy, a famous French harpist living during the reign of Louis XIV, felt that she owed her success largely to her cat, who was her sternest critic, and when she died she left her pampered puss a town house and a country home, plus plenty of money to pay the necessary carers at each address. Her relatives were not pleased but failed in their attempts to

RIGHT: *In the Middle Ages, a cat's stare was thought to be enough to put a spell on an enemy.*

contest the will. In modern times, rich owners have shown equal devotion to their feline friends. In 1991 American millionairess Terry Krumholz left her $750,000 Fifth Avenue home to her two cats, Damon and Pythias and in 1992 Beatrice Farrington left her luxurious fifty-roomed mansion in Connecticut to her seven-year-old cat Cyrus.

Myth and magic

Cats may have lost their sinister reputation but a whole body of 'cat lore' has gathered over the centuries and the myths and legends still linger in the twentieth century. Chief among them is the belief that cats have nine lives – nine because this is the most magical of numbers, a trinity of trinities. Cats probably earned this reputation for good fortune because of their ability to land on their feet and the agility which enables them to scoot out of danger, and there have certainly been a few felines who seemed intent on proving it true. Oscar was the ship's cat on the German battleship *Bismarck* in 1941 and when it was sunk he escaped, clinging with all claws to a piece of wreckage. He was spotted by the crew of the destroyer *Cossack* and hauled aboard but he had hardly had the chance to get used to his new home when the *Cossack*, too, became a casualty of war. This time he was picked up by the aircraft carrier *Ark Royal* but when the *Ark Royal* went down in its turn, some of the sailors risked their lives to save him and he was eventually landed in safety. He spent an honourable retirement at the Belfast Home for Sailors. Other cats have survived for astonishing lengths of time without sustenance. A black cat who stowed away in a car being exported from Britain to Australia emerged emaciated but alive after fifty days. Mercedes, named after the car, recovered in intensive care.

Certain cats are believed to be the bringers of good fortune: though in the UK black cats are considered lucky, in the USA they are thought unlucky and white is the favoured colour. Russians believe that, when moving into a new house, the family should take a cat in with them on

RIGHT: *Tales are told of cats surviving enormous hardship and danger, suggesting that they do, indeed, have nine lives.*

the first day and throw it onto the bed. If it has a wash and then settles down to sleep, the new home will be happy and prosperous. In China, many shops keep an indoor cat as a lucky charm and the older and uglier the cat, the more blessings it will bestow.

Special powers

At the time of the Roman empire, cats' faeces were mixed with mustard to cure external ulcers and with wine as a poultice to draw out thorns. At the time of the Great Fire of London, in 1666, the fur of skinned cats was used to treat burns, and in the Netherlands skins were wrapped round sore throats or eruptions of the skin. The Japanese believed that gastric ulcers and other gastric problems would be cured if a black cat lay across the stomach. In parts of Britain, the hair from a black cat's tail, drawn across the eyelid on the night of the full moon, was thought to be a certain cure for eye complaints. In *Tom Sawyer*, Mark Twain tells of the belief that warts could be cured by releasing a cat in a graveyard at dead of night after a burial because 'Devil follow corpse, cat follow Devil, wart follow cat'. Nowadays, cats are still seen as healers, with scientific backing. The very act of stroking a cat has been proved to reduce blood pressure and pulse rate. Research studies in the USA have shown that the survival rate among heart patients is higher for pet owners than for non-pet owners; a survey of 5,000 patients at the Baker Medical Research Institute showed that pet owners had significantly less risk of developing heart disease in the first place. On a less scientific level, many cat lovers maintain that just gazing into a cat's steady eyes will relieve stress.

One of the old myths about cats, particularly among fishermen, was that the pupils of their eyes reflected the state of the tides: closing into tiny slits meant that the tide was ebbing but wide black pupils meant high tide. How they explained that a cat's eyes can change from one state to the other every few minutes is not recorded! In several countries in the far East, cats are used to bring rain, being dunked in pools, doused with water or put into a river to swim ashore. In eastern Europe they are thought to attract lightning – an echo of the old belief that cats were possessed by devils and God sent the lightning to purge the evil spirits

RIGHT: *In the UK black cats are thought to be lucky, while in the US they are believed to bring misfortune.*

– and are chased well away from the house during thunderstorms. The cat's sensitivity to changes in atmospheric conditions was held, in more superstitious times, as proof that they had power to change the weather. Now we realise that though a cat may wash over the tops of its ears when rain is on the way, sit with its back to the fire when cold weather is coming or dash about madly when storms and high winds are due, this only means that it can sense these changes more quickly than we do.

Homing cats

There is plenty of argument among experts about the phenomenon of 'psi-trailing', when cats find their way home over enormous distances, in territory they could never have travelled before. In 1988 a French cat called Gribouille made headlines after a 1,000 km (620 mile) journey from south-west Germany to central France. His owner, Madame Martinet, had given him to a neighbour just before he moved to Germany but Gribouille refused to settle in his new home and after three weeks he disappeared. Nearly two years later he turned up on Madame Martinet's doorstep, thin, bedraggled and sickly. Obviously he had changed out of all recognition but his mother knew him immediately and busily began cleaning him up. Once he was clean and fed, Gribouille, who still answered to his name, made straight for his favourite spot in a patch of herbs under a plum tree. A Persian cat called Howie accomplished an even more amazing feat by walking a distance of 1,600 km (1,000 miles) across the rugged Australian outback. The Hicks family had left him with relatives while they made an extended trip abroad but Howie was having none of it. He set off for his home in Adelaide and arrived there a year later. Stories of cats travelling several hundred kilometres to return to their homes are too numerous to tell.

Various explanations have been given for this homing ability, one being that the cat might be able to navigate by the exact position of the sun and stars in relation to its home, but experiments in an enclosed maze without these natural aids, showed that cats had an instinct for choosing the exit that pointed towards their home. Some scientists think that they are especially sensitive to the earth's magnetic

FACING PAGE: *There are several well-known cases of cats that have found their way home over enormous distances.*

LEFT: *Fearless hunters one moment and purring companions the next, cats are always fascinating.*

field, like an animal compass, for they find that a magnet attached to the cat's collar will interfere with its homing instincts.

No convincing explanation has been found for cats who apparently manage to follow their owners to a new home, in an area they have never seen, like Sugar, the Californian cat. When his owners moved to Oklahoma, they left him with a neighbour, convinced that he would be happier staying on familiar territory. Sugar disagreed and 13 months later he turned up at his family's farm in Oklahoma, 2,414 km (1,500 miles) from where he started. Sceptics claim that such cat reunions are only wishful thinking. They maintain that a stray cat of similar size and colour, arriving on the doorstep and eager for a home, is only too happy to answer to any name and conform to any family pattern – then the owner's imagination does the rest. It's an explanation that cat-lovers will always find hard to swallow. We still like to think that there's something just a little bit magical about a cat.

Index